Washing & Caring For Your Motorcycle

by Al Scott

A BigScotty.com Publication

1st Edition

BIG SCOTTY

Table of Contents

LEGAL DISCLAIMER

Biker's Prayer

May your belly
never grumble

May your clutch
never break

May your ride
never tumble

May your rear
never ache

PREFACE

Ever since I bought my first motorcycle back in 1970, I have enjoyed washing and detailing bikes. There's something satisfying about doing that work yourself. Sometimes you just can't find the time. I get that. Sometimes you may be in a situation where you make more money than the detailer and you can't afford to take time off. I get that too.

But if you can wash or detail your own motorcycle, chances are you'll get lots of personal satisfaction from your hard work. There's nothing like the feeling you get when heads turn as your freshly cleaned motorcycle drives by.

There's another very important reason to wash/detail your bike regularly. It forces you to be in constant contact with your machine. That means it is much more likely you will notice the occasional loose wire, nut, bolt, etc. Safety is a plenty good excuse to go wash your motorcycle.

Whatever your purpose or reason for washing and caring for your motorcycle, I hope this book helps you do it more quickly, more efficiently, more safely, more effectively, and more cost efficiently.

Our motorcycles are often among our biggest assets. So it makes sense to protect them. Maintaining your bike's appearance just makes sense financially, and it's fun.

Fun is the best reason to take care of your bike. Most of all, I hope you have fun and get better results than you were getting before you read the book. Believe it or not, I find cleaning my bike to be one of the most enjoyable, relaxing things I can do - other than riding it of course.

Let me know what you think of the book. Is there something important I missed? What topic(s) would you like to see covered in my next book on motorcycle appearance? Send me an email. My address is simple - scotty@bigscotty.com.

Thank you and best wishes, Big Scotty

INTRODUCTION

Much of the material in this book can be applied to washing/detailing ANY vehicle. Do be careful and pay attention to the safety warnings throughout the book. The last thing I want to see happen is someone getting hurt due to carelessness or the misapplication of the information I've provided here.

With that out of the way, I want you to notice a few things. This book is pretty basic. I'm not going very deep into many of the chapters because frankly, unless you plan to wash/detail motorcycles for a living, there's no need. I've provided more than enough information for you to get your bike looking great. If you want to go deeper, I suggest that you purchase a course in vehicle detailing or attend a detailing school. It's a fun and easy way to make a living, as long as you like washing bikes as much as I do.

I also want you to note that I've been very specific in my product recommendations. Hopefully you noticed that I didn't blindly recommend every single product that Mothers, or Meguiars Car Care or any other company makes. That's because I don't believe any one company makes all the perfect products. You have to mix and match to find out what works best for you. I've tried to save you some leg work by testing most of the major products on the market. It's my opinion that the products I select and endorse below are the best for the application intended with an eye toward getting the best result, with the least amount of money or time invested.

Also note I am not sponsored by any of these companies. My opinions are my own and not for sale. Please keep this in mind when you read other books or manuals on vehicle detailing. Many of those books are written by professional detailers who are getting paid to sell a product. I am not. I'm selecting the best tools and materials I can find without regard for brand preference.

I hope this distinction gives you the confidence you need to trust in my recommendations. But of course, you should always feel free to investigate and test other products. You may find that for you personally, product x works better than product y. Choose what's best for you. The tools really do matter, but it's the technique and love of motorcycling that can set your results apart more quickly than the most expensive tools.

CHAPTER ONE - PREPPING YOURSELF TO WASH YOUR MOTORCYCLE

"Life is short. Bend the rules, forgive quickly, love honestly, laugh easily, keep it simple, ride often, ride free and never regret anything that makes you smile."

I know that many reading this will think I am advocating overkill, but I have enough experience (having detailed more than 100 motorcycles in my life) to know that there is no such thing as overkill when it comes to being prepared to properly wash and detail a motorcycle.

You wouldn't believe how many little things can go wrong and ruin your day if you are unprepared. I have a check list that I quickly run down before I start washing and detailing a motorcycle.

First of all, I go without a belt or wear pants that hide the belt buckle. Nothing like bending over and scratching the paint due to your own stupidity. And do you use reading glasses? Make sure you get an eyeglass head band to hold them on your head. Also don't store them in your pocket. They fall off or out and boom - just like that another scratch to attend to.

Also remove rings, watches and any other metal pieces on your person that might scratch the bike. Don't wear anything with an exposed zipper.

I generally like to make sure I have NOTHING in my pockets. No wallets, combs, pocket protectors full of pens, no cell phone! (You can actually do without your cell phone for a whole hour. Go ahead and try it. Nothing bad will happen. The earth will continue to rotate. The sun will go up in the morning and down at night. Really!)

Next I make sure I am wearing a buttonless shirt (T-Shirt) or a shop shirt which hides the shirt buttons.

I also like to wear shoes with a solid grip. If you slip and fall into the bike and knock it over - you'll be unhappy. Trust me. It happened to me and I am STILL unhappy.

I wear rubber gloves when using certain chemicals and thin mechanics gloves the rest of the time. If you wash or detail bikes often this is a life-saver. You can avoid damaging your skin or getting small cuts and bruises from sticking your hands inside the frame to reach those hard to reach engine spots or wheels, etc.

I like to wear old motorcycle boots when I wash my bike. They have good grip but if you drop something heavy on them they offer pretty good protection. It's also okay if they get wet.

If you're going to be using a buffer or other motorized equipment (such as a vacuum or generator) make sure you also have ear protection. Ear plugs are cheap. Visits to the Ear/Nose/Throat doctor - not so much.

Eye protection is also high on my list. You don't need those dorky safety glasses you wore in shop class (although they work fine.) But some sort of clear safety glasses, tied around your head, will protect your eyes in the event that the chemicals you use spill or react in some way that causes them to find your eyeballs. I actually know a guy who was partially blinded by an acid-based wheel cleaner he was using. When he applied the cleaner it came out of the bottle faster than he expected and the back flush hit him in the right eye. Safety glasses cost $5.00. Buy them and use them. Your vision is worth a whole lot more.

I also like to have a set of knee pads nearby. If you're doing a lot of kneeling, your knees will thank you in 20 years if you take care of them now.

CHAPTER TWO - PREPPING YOUR WORK AREA

"Ever want to know why dogs like to stick their heads out of the car window? Ask a biker."

It seems like a small thing, but having the right work area can mean the difference between a great bike cleanup and a horrible bike cleanup. You want to make sure the area is safe, legal, free of objects that can impede your movement around the bike, free of objects that can fall on the bike, and free of obstructions to walkways and passages where other people need to get by.

INDOORS

If you can wash your bike indoors, this is ideal. You want a cool, dry place to work in. The area will be less dusty and you can control the lighting and surrounding circumstances. A garage is a typical place to wash the motorcycle. But prepping the garage for this event takes some thought. Move all vehicles (other than the motorcycle you are cleaning) out of the garage. Remove ladders, bicycles, and anything that can fall or that you might bump into causing it to fall onto the bike.

Make sure the garage itself is as clean as can be before you bring the bike in. Sweep and mop the garage floor for best results. That way dust, dirt and lint that's laying on the garage floor will not transfer to the bike.

Try to make as much room for yourself and your bike as you possibly can. The more room you have to work with, the better off you will be.

Check with your local municipality to see if it allows indoor vehicle washes. Some cities require that you use a water reclaimer (for environmental reasons) so make sure you know your local laws. In places where there are such laws, there are usually rental garages that have water reclaimers you can rent by the hour for a nominal fee.

OUTDOORS

Sometimes you just can't wash/detail your bike indoors. In that case, assuming it violates no local laws, finding a big open park with lots of shade is probably your best bet. (Shade doesn't mean you have to be UNDER the tree full of birds making bird poop. It just means you have to be somewhere that shade is available.)

Make sure you park in an area that is free of debris. Also note whether or not you have to ride by a bunch of water sprinklers when you leave the park. There's nothing worse than investing a solid hour in polishing your baby only to have the lawn sprinklers come on as you ride by.

Don't park too close to the curb since you will need room to work around both wheels.

ASSEMBLE YOUR TOOLS

Once you have your area ready, get everything that you might need gathered into one, easily-accessible place. It makes sense to put everything close so you don't have to waste time going back and forth gathering supplies.

CHAPTER THREE - PREPPING YOUR MOTORCYCLE

"Owning a motorcycle is not a matter of life or death. It's much more important than that. Live to ride or step aside."

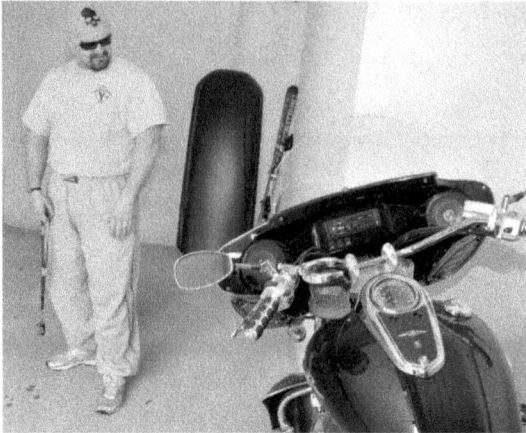

It's time to address the bike. First off, make sure your bike is cool. I like the 90-minute rule. Let the bike sit 90 minutes after riding it so the engine, pipes, etc. are cool to the touch. (Your mileage may vary. Test your bike to see where the cool down point is. Don't rely on my rule. Make up your own.) Next, you want to protect any sophisticated electronics. Also protect your gauges, carb, open air filters, breather and seat. Also protect any leather surface. Protect the exhaust tips so water can't get into your pipes.

I use plastic wrap, small plastic bags and painter's tape for these jobs. All are readily available at any supermarket or hardware store.

Can you skip this step? Sure. Your bike gets wet when it rains. But remember that the less water it is exposed to the better, and riding tends to put the bike in a situation where it's blowing off the water. Washing a bike lets the water pool and may cause damage. At the very least, it will add wear and tear.

Another step you should consider if you want to seriously clean the motorcycle is getting it off the ground. This can be accomplished using any number of motorcycle lifts ranging in price from $100-$600. Using a lift usually allows the wheels to turn freely which makes them much easier to clean. NOTE: for safety reasons, you might want to have a second person available to help load a motorcycle onto a lift.

Lastly, if you want the most extreme detail possible remove parts like fairings, windshields, saddlebags and anything else that will get in the way of cleaning ALL of the motorcycle. You can solve this problem by buying purified water in five-gallon buckets, using a water softener (I just use my home water softener and attach my hose directly to it) or you can buy a portable unit that uses salt/resin to purify the water. These units are widely available from RV and camping stores and good ones cost between $150 and $400. Having good, clean water is a must. There's no reason to touch the bike if you plan to use hard water because it leaves spots that can actually damage your paint. The bike's better off dirty.

CHAPTER FOUR - MOTORCYCLE WASHING / DETAILING TOOLS / SUPPLIES

"There are two types of people in this world, people who ride motorcycles and people who wish they could ride motorcycles."

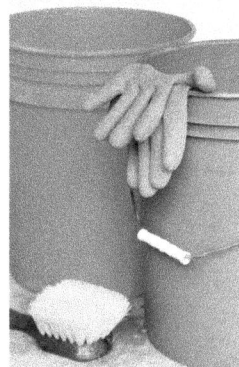

I'm going to spend a lot of time covering the various supplies and tools you will need to take care of your bike because this is where the rubber meets the road - pun intended. You can end up saving or costing yourself a whole bunch of time depending on whether or not you have the right tools and supplies.

You can probably make do with just about anything you have around the house if all you want is a basic bike wash. But the problem is that if you use cheap or incorrect materials, you can actually cause permanent damage to the bike's finish. It's better to take the time to study the proper materials and more importantly to understand why you need them and how they make a difference.

Let's start with some simple concepts and axioms. The cheap stuff is cheap for a reason. It may do the job, and there are a few very good inexpensive products. But the old adage "you get what you pay for" applies particularly well when it comes to motorcycle washing/detailing products. If you just don't have the money, then go to WalMart and buy the general car care brands like Mothers or Meguiar's and be done with it. You can't buy the professional quality stuff there. You can only get the consumer strength products. But if budget is a significant issue, then by all means stick with name brands and buy them at the cheapest place you can find.

But then again - few people reading this book are in that situation. Few people NEED a motorcycle. Most motorcycle sales go to people who use the bikes in a recreational manner. Some very small percentage of motorcycle owners (in the USA anyway) depend on motorcycles for their sole means of transportation. That means, if you have the discretionary income to buy a bike, you probably have the money needed to step up to the best quality detailing supplies. (Note I cover towels and wash mitts, etc., in chapter five.)

I am going to start by covering some basics. This is best accomplished by warning you about some common misconceptions and mistakes.

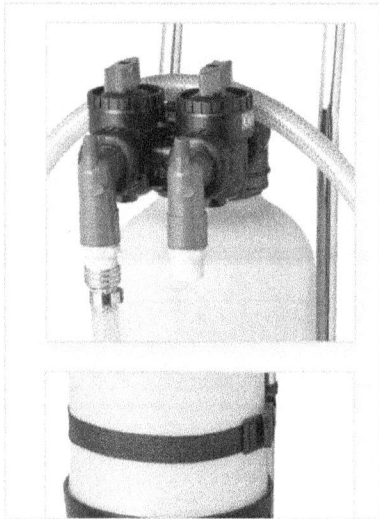

1. Do NOT use hard water to "wash" your bike. Hard water is pretty much any water that isn't purified. Depending on where you live, you may have really hard water or darn near perfect water, but most places lean towards the really bad water side. The solution can be something as simple as having a plumber run an extra line off your water softener. Other options include buying water (like the mobile car wash people do.) This requires that you have a large 20 gallon or larger tank to store the water in. An easy solution if you can afford it is a portable water deionizer such as this one from Griot's Garage.

http://bit.ly/1dipAVT

2. Make sure your work area is free of debris, objects that could fall or that you could bump into causing them to fall. Make sure you have good access to the bike. One of the best ways to do this is invest in a motorcycle jack. For less than $150 I like the ATD Tools 7461 Motorcycle/ATV Jack. I am not positive but I am pretty sure this is nearly identical to the jack Harley Davidson sells for twice the price. It's sturdy, can be operated by one person (although it's always best to have two people when you jack up a bike,) and it's solid as a rock. Using a jack lets you get better access to the wheels and tires and underside of the engine.

http://amzn.to/1bsH1n0

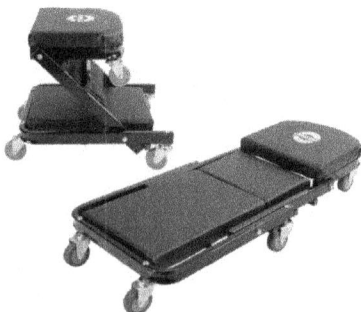

3. Get yourself a small rolling caddie, cart or stool. This way you can propel yourself around the bike while sitting down. Occasionally you'll want to crawl under the bike so a rolling stool and combination creeper is the best bet. I like the Omega 91000 Black 40" Foldable Z Creeper for this task.

http://amzn.to/IBrQhC

4. When you need to spray water on your bike, you'll either want a professional pressure washer or a commercial quality hose and reel. You'll also want a good quality nozzle for your hose with variable pressure. For nozzles, my hands-down favorite is the Nelson 50503 High-Pressure Rated Fireman's Style Industrial Spray Nozzle with Large On/Off Lever.

http://amzn.to/19cRe7B

For hoses, length is a consideration. The shorter the hose, the easier it is to manage. Most people can get by with 25 feet. Some will need 50 or even 100 feet. You also may want a lead-free solution, both because several states have legislated against lead in consumer products, and because the lead in the hose can make the water hard on your bike. I've tried every commercial grade garden hose you can buy and have had the best results with the Water Right PSH-025-MG-6PKRS 25-Foot x 1/2-Inch Polyurethane Lead Safe Ultra Light Slim Garden Hose.

http://amzn.to/18PGdLF

If you want an alternative hose I also like the Gilmour 10 Series 8 Ply Flexogen Hose 1/2 inch #10.

http://amzn.to/1gTxQhM

You'll need hoses even if you go with a pressure washer. If you do buy a pressure washer you can spend between $100 and $2000 on such a unit. I've found little difference between the high-end pressure washers and those designed for home use. I think you should be able to keep the cost of a pressure washer under $300 pretty easily. My pick is the Snow Joe Sun Joe SPX3000 2030 PSI 1.76 GPM Electric Pressure Washer, 14.5-Amp.

http://amzn.to/1fe0qdc

5. Shampoo/Car Washes/Bike Washes come in a variety of forms but my experience has taught me that the formulas based on biodegradable polymers offer the best bang for the buck. I use Optimum Car Wash. It is very concentrated, does not strip wax, foams well to flood away the grime, and rinses completely in cold water. It is environmentally safe.

Oh and don't let the name fool you. It works great on motorcycles too!

http://amzn.to/1f2nriu

Another way to do this is with a rinseless carwash product. This uses only two small buckets of water, and a special chemical designed to accomplish much of what you would do with a traditional car wash. Key to making this system work is the right chemical. Hands down Adams new Rinseless car wash is the best I've tried. It's very powerful and concentrated. Use one bucket with two ounces of this product diluted into clean water and another bucket with just clean water. Have at least two, large, fluffy, high-quality micro fiber towels. Use one bucket to suds up one of the towels and just wipe on the product in one straight edge-to-edge motion. Then come behind it with the clean towel to dry. Repeat over each section of the bike. It works 90% as well as a regular car wash unless your bike has lots of grease, mud, etc.

http://bit.ly/1jFZPns

6. If you have to remove grease, gum, tar, sap or any other sticky substance the surefire cure is Tarminator Bug/Tar/Sap/Grease Remover. Follow the directions carefully and you'll have zero problems. NOTE: This stuff is highly flammable so be careful with it. If you're a smoker set your pack of Camels down before you apply Tarminator.

http://amzn.to/1gU7oo4

7. After you put water on your bike, you'll need to take it off. Rather than spending 20 minutes hand drying (and possibly scratching the finish) just blow off the water. The other advantage of using an air blower to take water off the bike is that it prevents water from pooling in hard to reach places. These pools of water can lead to rust and other paint damage. Get the water off first with an air blower then touch up with micro fiber towels. My favorite air blower for these kinds of jobs is the Air force Master Blaster. You can also use a garden variety (pun intended) leaf blower but be sure to cover the tip with a mesh material that stops debris contained inside the blower from blowing onto your paint.

http://amzn.to/19eVdAI

And here's a pro tip. For the very hard to reach, small, tight areas, I use simple canned compressed air. Any brand will do, but my choice is good old Dust Off. It's ozone safe and just works.

I use Dust Off to blow out the radio speakers on my Street Glide. I also use it to force air into small compartments in the batwing fairing like the iPhone/iPod cubby hole. Depending on the bike you're washing, there are many places this comes in handy.

http://amzn.to/1bTXAeh

8. If your bike has a headlight or fairing you may need glass cleaner. (This also works brilliantly to shine up (not polish) chrome.) Look no further than Sonax 338241-755 Clear/Green Glass Cleaner for an amazing and affordable glass cleaner. NOTE: If you're working in very warm temperatures, most glass cleaners streak. It's just something you can't avoid. Try applying as little product as you can and use a special micro fiber towel designed for glass. You can get the glass clean in 100 plus degree heat but you may not be able to avoid a few minor streaks.

http://amzn.to/1kvV9hB

9. You may need to vacuum dirt, dust and debris from your bike (or just from your garage where you wash the bike.) If you have the Metro Vacuum I recommended that might be all you need. But there's nothing like a wall-mounted system that stays out of your way if you want to go top-shelf. Rather than dragging around a vacuum cleaner, tripping over it or the power cable, try a wall-mounted unit. I use the Hoover GUV ProGrade Garage Utility Vacuum. It's the most powerful, effective solution in its price range.

http://amzn.to/19f0gB3

I like to use separate units for vacuuming and blowing. That's why I have both the Metro AND the Hoover.

10. When you buy chemicals, you save a whole bunch of money if you buy bulk sizes and then mix down into your own spray bottles. This way you can handle them in more manageable quantities. You will need some spray bottles. I don't like the cheap bottles you buy in the hardware store. You need heavy duty, chemical-resistant bottles and these will last you four times as long as the cheap ones, but they don't cost four times as much. My favorite is Chemical Guys Super Heavy-Duty Chemical Resistant Sprayer w/ Bottle.

http://amzn.to/1aSa2Fk

11. If you own a motorcycle, eventually you'll have to polish your chrome. There are lots of products out there that claim to be the best. I've tested all of them. Even some available only in Europe. Bang for the buck, the Mothers Billet Metal Polish is the best product I've used to restore chrome that's pitted, discolored etc. It takes some elbow grease and for best results use a buffer, but nothing else comes close and remains safe.

http://amzn.to/1dmmNLs

12. When you're dealing with boot marks, road tar and other nasty stuff that adheres to your bike's exhaust pipes, even the Mothers Billet Metal Polish won't always work.

There are lots of home remedies for this - including the old standby - Easy Off Oven Cleaner, but they don't always work. If you want guaranteed results every time you need an absolutely magical product called Kleen King Hot Pipes Exhaust Cleaner. Be careful since the pipes are hot I suggest wearing thick mechanics gloves when applying the product.

Apply the product liberally and wipe it off. It may take a little rubbing with a thick micro fiber cloth but it always, always, always works for me.

http://amzn.to/1fgWSH4

13. If you want to address scratches (minor scratches) then you will need a buffer. There are lots of misconceptions about buffers and there is no doubt that if you buy the wrong one, and misuse it, you can and probably will cause more damage than you started with. So buy the right buffer, invest 20 minutes in watching free videos on how to use it, and you'll have no problem. For beginners I recommend two different orbital buffers. These won't burn your paint and are very manageable and affordable. I recommend two sizes because the larger size may be overkill for some motorcycles, especially if you don't want to have to strip off your fenders, tank, saddle bags, etc., to get to small, hard-to-reach areas. I have listed both below. Note I suggest the 25' cord. It gives you more wiggle room and as long as you remember to always, always, always drape it over your shoulder, it won't be a problem. NOTE: Some "detailing snobs" as I like to call them will trash these simple random orbiters. But trust me when I tell you they work just fine. Unless you've had professional training, you wouldn't likely get anything more out of the high-quality, powerful buffers made by companies like Flex. These are great tools but in the wrong hands, can do more harm than good. Let the snobs be snobs and know that you can do 95% of the paint correction you need with the tools below. Even though I've had lots of training, practice and experience, I still prefer the random orbital buffers. After all, since I detail other people's bikes as well as my own, I don't like taking chances.

There are more than two dozen well-known power machines you can use for detailing/ cleaning your motorcycle. But for the beginner, there are only two you need to worry about.

For larger areas like gas tanks and saddlebags, I use:

Griot's Garage 10813LNGCRD 6" Random Orbital with 25' Cord

http://amzn.to/IDescU

For smaller areas like side covers and hard to reach places, I use:

Griot's Garage 10739LNGCRD 3" Random Orbital with 25' Cord

http://amzn.to/IDefGH

You can buy an assortment of pads and polishes from Griots that are designed to work with their orbital polishers, and I recommend that you do. *Match the pad, and the polish to the buffer.* You can find both the products (along with some very valuable training videos) at the Griotsgarage web site - http://www.griotsgarage.com. Note that this is a hobbyist solution. If you plan on becoming a professional detailer you'll eventually need formal training in polishing with a machine. But short of that, these random orbital buffers work very well and most importantly, very safely.

14. After you wash but before you polish or wax, you should clay bar. Adam's Made in the USA Detailing Clay is effective, user friendly, and affordable. It comes with some detailing spray, which is necessary to properly work the clay bar on the paint surface. The clay bar removes small imperfections in the paint's surface. These imperfections are usually something you can feel when you run your hand over the painted surfaces on the motorcycle.

It takes practice to get this right, so start with a small area of the bike. If the clay bar grabs, you aren't using enough lubricant (in the form of the spray detailer.) If it's not picking up imperfections in the paint, you're using too much lubricant. You'll get a feel for it if you spend 15 minutes experimenting.

http://amzn.to/1bAtD1d

15. A good sealant can make your bike look better than new. It also has the very important job of protecting your paint. If you go to all the trouble of washing, clay barring, etc., you'll have wasted your effort if you don't finish off with a good sealant.

If you're on a budget, (and if you don't want to use a buffer to apply your sealant) nothing I've tried in this price category works as well as Nanoskin NA-NSE16 Nano Shock Instant Lubricant Sealant.

http://amzn.to/1fh0QPK

If you want the very best, and can afford the money and the time to apply it, 22PLE, VX1 Signature Glass Coat is hands down the most amazing product I've ever used on any vehicle.

It's hard to find, and is typically only sold to professional detailers, but if you can get your hands on it - you'll love it. It literally applies a glass coating above your clear coat. It's a professional-grade product so paying very strict, close attention to the application directions is imperative. It's not hard, but you do have to follow the direction. 22PLE will protect paint for up to two years. Water not only beads up off this coating, it simply never hangs around long enough to stick. Gum, tar, all sorts of road debris will wipe right off if you use this coating. Be aware it needs five days to dry and you have to be able to keep your bike out of the rain for five consecutive days to make sure in bonds properly to the clear coat. (At the time of this writing VX1 was available at http://www.esotericcarcare.com.)

16. I'm not a big fan of waxes as you'll see below, but if I use a wax, I don't want to spend a fortune on it, and I don't want to work my butt off applying it. Meguiar's NXT Generation Tech Wax 2.0 is affordable, easy-to-use, and because of its polymer base, very effective, especially for the money. It's easy to put on and comes off just as easily without residue. It's also one of the few wax products that you don't need a buffer to apply. You can literally spray this stuff on, wipe it off, and get a deep, wet, shine on your paint.

http://amzn.to/1bugORN

The bottom line for this section of the book is simple. Buy quality products. There's a reason that the good stuff costs a little bit more. In most cases it's worth it, and it can extend the life of your motorcycle's finish.

CHAPTER FIVE MICRO-FIBER TOWELS

"Saddlebags can never hold everything you want, but they CAN hold everything you need."

You may think it odd that I've devoted an entire chapter to micro-fibre towels but they are one of the most important components of any competent bike wash or detail. I'll point out some of my favorite towels below.

I'm going to cover three things in this chapter.

1. Why you should use micro-fiber towels

2. How to pick the right micro-fibre towel

3. How to properly use a micro-fibre towel

1. Why you should use micro fiber towels

Micro fiber towels are diverse. They can accomplish many jobs. You can use them to wash, dry and apply wax or polish. They are better than terry cloth or cotton in most cases because they don't leave lint behind. They are also much less prone to leave scratches or towel marks when used properly.

2. How to pick the right micro fiber towel

This is the one place that I think you should splurge. Buy the best micro fiber towels you can possibly afford. The right towel can save you time, effort and even money. The wrong towel can do the opposite. Don't cheap out when you buy your micro fiber towels.

Look for towels that are 16x16." This is the perfect size for most bike washing/detailing jobs. Also look for towels without tags (or tags you can easily remove) and towels without edges that can scratch. I like absorbent towels that can be machine washed.

3. How to properly use a micro-fibre towel

You should know that while very soft, even something as soft as a micro fiber towel can put scratches and swirl marks into your paint. Since we don't want to have to learn how to buff those out just yet, it's better not to put them into the paint in the first place.

The basic thing to know is to start with a clean towel. I have a 1-2-3 rule when it comes to micro fibre towels. I never use a towel more than three times on my bike. The first time is for pristine paint work. The second time is for drying or working on non-painted surfaces and the third time is for things like chrome, wheels, engines or anything that carries lots of grease and grime.

Is this expensive? You bet. But so is a new coat of paint.

The next thing to know about your micro fiber towel is that it works best when damp or wet. Never put a towel on a car without first applying some small amount of product like quick detailing spray, etc. Without lubrication, the most plush towel can leave a mark.

Start by folding the towel into quarters. Never use a flat towel on a good paint surface. It is a surefire way to leave swirls. Instead, fold the towel over into quarters. Constantly turn the towel inside out and around to make sure you're always working with a clean surface. You should work on small areas. Most people get into trouble because they try to do too much at once. Think small. One half of the front fender might be a good example. One half of one side of the front fender would even be better. Work small and you'll get big results.

Don't apply too much pressure. If you're using the right chemicals (i.e., the ones I recommend) then you shouldn't have to work so hard to get product on or off the bike. Apply minimal pressure to avoid scratches. Try to wipe in a constant direction. Micro fibre towels work best when you don't rub them back and forth over the same area. Because of the way they capture dirt, dust, debris, chemicals etc., wiping both directions can simply have the effect of wiping back on what you just wiped off.

Apply product with one side of the towel and buff it off with the other. You get into a rhythm of folding the towel four-ways flat, turning it, pulling it inside out, etc., and you get the best results. Change towels often and your results will improve.

I also want to share a note about caring for micro fiber towels. A good laundry detergent and hot water is the best way to wash your towels. Bleach is harsh and wears on the fibers of your towels. You could divide dirty towels into heavy-duty grime and regular grime. You'll probably want to prewash the dirtiest towels using special degreasers or cleaners. Then wash the lightly soiled towels separately. Pre-washed towels could be added to the lightly soiled towels after they've gone through a pre-wash to remove the worst tar, bug residue, and oil. Don't use fabric softener because it will reduce the absorbency of your towels.

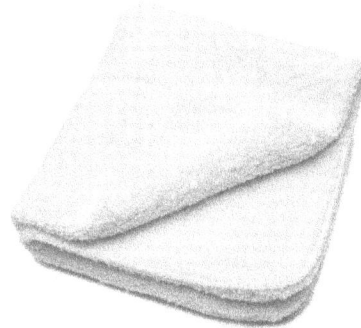

For washing the bike I like to use a wash mitt. Griot's Garage makes a nice, affordable micro fiber wash mitt that holds more water than sheepskin and won't scratch your paint. It's also machine washable.

http://bit.ly/1jKrFik

A great all-purpose towel is the Chemical Guys White 16" x 16" Edgeless Microfiber Polishing Towel. They are expensive but well worth it. They have no edge and are not going to scratch your paint surface. They remove chemical product without streaks.

http://amzn.to/1dnn1lH

CHAPTER SIX WASHING YOUR BIKE

"Sometimes it takes a whole tank of fuel before you can think straight."

You've done all the prep work, gathered the best chemicals and tools you can afford, you've found the perfect place to work, now all you have to do is actually wash the bike.

Proper washing, rinsing, and drying techniques safely remove dirt and road grime and set the stage for a show-bike shine free of spots and scratches.

First things first. Let the bike cool off before washing. Not only is it safer for you, it avoids water spots and can prevent more serious damage like cracked engine heads. Also make sure you're using room temperature, clean water from a water purifying system. (Don't use HOT water.) Use the right chemicals such as one of the wash solutions mentioned above. Do NOT use dish soap since it can harm your finish, and if you have waxes or polishes on your bike, dish soap may remove these protections. Seriously, this is one of the worst things you can do to your bike's finish.

Check out your bike and examine the condition of the exterior surfaces, wheels, and tires. Depending on how soiled it is, you'll be able to decide which products you'll want to use. For example, if you see bug splatters, tar, or pitch, you'll want to be sure to grab special cleaners.

Next, assemble your tools and prepare your buckets of water. Some people like to use one bucket for cleaning tires and wheels and two buckets (one soapy and one rinse water) to wash the car. As you wash, use the rinse bucket to rinse off your wash mitt before you dip it back into the soapy water. This reduces the chances of grit from your initial pass marring the paint job as you continue to clean the car. A Grit Guard is a handy tool for keeping grit at the bottom of your wash bucket. It keeps the dirt and grime settled at the bottom.

I prefer to use a wash mitt to clean the bike. Some people like micro fibre cloths and some use pure cotton cloths. Whatever you do - never use a brush - no matter how soft, on any painted surface on the bike. Brushes are for wheels, tires, and engines, and that's all. Never use anything like a T-shirt; it acts like sandpaper on dirty surfaces.

Whatever tool you use to wash the bike, remember, this is another place you shouldn't try to save money. Buy the good stuff and when it's worn out, replace it - which will be often. If you start with a dirty wash mitt then the rest of the job is a waste of time.

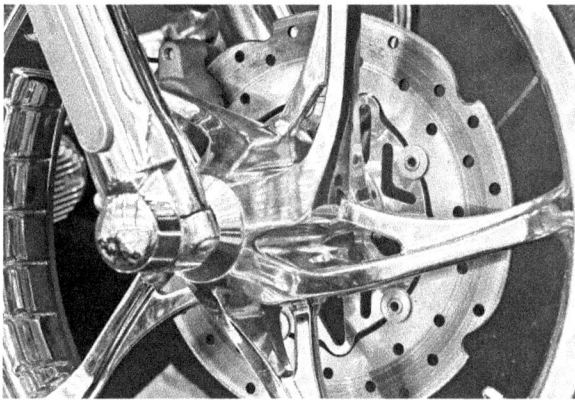

I like to start with tires and wheels. Spotless shiny wheels are one standout feature of a pro-level shine. And giving your wheels some extra attention will protect them. Brake dust has a way of deteriorating wheels over time if they aren't cleaned regularly.

Know your wheel type. Before you clean, make sure to know what material your wheels are made out of or coated with so that you can safely clean them with the proper product. Wheels can be polished aluminum, uncoated metal, factory painted, chrome, and anodized. Factory paint is a harder and more corrosion resistant coating than your car's regular paint. If your car's wheels are clear coated, no color residue should come off on a towel, and you'll want to be careful not to use harsh metal cleaners on a clear-coated wheel.

To know for sure what your wheels are made of, check with the manufacturer or the dealership to determine exactly what it is and how to best clean and protect it.

Chrome wheels are corrosion resistant and can handle stronger cleaners and will withstand dirt and road grime without deteriorating,, as long as you're consistent about keeping them clean.

Bare metal wheels will oxidize over time. You'll know if this is what you have if you wipe them with cleaner and your towel turns gray or dirty looking. Using wheel cleaners that are safe for uncoated wheels can ensure you're doing the right and safe thing to maintain your wheels.

Techniques: Work on one tire and wheel at a time. Begin by spraying the wheel, wheel well, and tire with water to wash off brake dust, road grime and dirt. Spray all-purpose or wheel cleaner onto the wheel and tire. Use a soft brush to clean behind and around the wheel into the wheel well, taking care to avoid scrubbing too hard on any areas that are painted. Rinse off the brush each time you use it so you don't transfer dirt and grime from one wheel to the next. (Remember a harsh brush can damage wheels so be careful to select one that won't scratch the wheel surface.)

Next, spray the wheel and calipers with wheel cleaner. Let it sit on the tire as directed on the package. Scrub it with a soft lug brush and rinse the brush, then spray another coating of wheel cleaner on the wheel and scrub with a softer bristle brush. Repeat this process with both wheels.

Note: It isn't advisable to let cleaning fluids dry on the wheel, in particular for polished aluminum and other materials. You want the chemicals off but don't worry about finishing the wheels now. When you wash the rest of the bike, they will get wet again and that's okay. You'll finish them off after you do the rest of the motorcycle.

You'll note I am breaking down sections of the bike. Work from the top down. This may seem like common sense but in my nearly six decades on this planet I've found there's nothing common about sense. Working from the top down lets all the chemicals and water fall down on the bike so you're able to clean those areas on the way down - naturally.

Pre-spray any areas that show bugs or tar, etc. Then rinse. Then wash. Spray the car with water again to prepare for the wash. Prepare a bike wash solution of water and shampoo. The directions on your shampoo bottle will provide a good guide to the ratio of shampoo and water to use. As you wash, dip your mitt into the soapy water without wringing it out and gently swipe it across the panels. Be gentle to avoid scratching the paint.

Then it's time to rinse. After you've thoroughly washed the bike, rinse the entire vehicle from top to bottom.

I like to wash and rinse each section of the bike independently. That way the harsh chemicals in the soap don't sit on the bike too long. I usually use two buckets. One with soapy (treated) water and one with fresh (treated) water. I use one mitt to apply the soap and one mitt to wipe it off, keeping each mitt in its respective bucket. Whatever you use, prevent dirt particles from damaging your paint, by regularly rinsing your rag/mitt/ sponge in a separate bucket before dipping it back into the soap when removing loose contaminants.

If you use a spray washer use a low pressure setting. High pressure spray washers can damage your motorcycle.

(A bucket dolly - like the one that comes from Pinnacle) is a handy way to keep your buckets moving with you around the bike. Putting the buckets on wheels makes the day go faster.)

http://amzn.to/19fQZJ3

For bikes with lots of stubborn dirt, mud, or grease I use a hose and a spray nozzle. I use a low-power pressure washer (Remember never use high power pressure washers to wash any part of your bike, especially the engine or any place there might be an intake or electronics.)

Blow dry the bike first, getting water out of all the hidden places. It's important to quickly dry your bike before water drops dry and leave spots. Use clean towels or chamois to remove the majority of water from your motorcycle. Then use a micro fiber weave pattern towel to dry the bike. You can use professional squeegees to do this job but since the painted surfaces on a bike are minimal, it's overkill. Dry carefully with clean towels to avoid contaminants that would scratch the finish. Blot or wipe gently. Don't use the same towel to dry the bike as you do to apply polishes and waxes. Remember that water you're soaking up is dirty. If you re-use that towel you will put the dirt right back on the bike.

If the bike is in good shape, you can just use standard detailer's glass cleaner or detail spray to make the chrome pieces look neat and shiny. If you have dirt on your pipes or worse, boot marks, etc., then you will need to clean and polish the chrome using any of the chemicals/methods mentioned in the tools section. Note: You should start with the least abrasive method and work up from there. Use a special soft micro fiber cloth for this and make sure it's clean. Don't re-use any towel you've used to wash the bike.

This is also a great time to remove any bugs, tar, chewing gum, etc. from the bike that didn't come off during the wash. In my experience Tarminator (see above) is perfect for this and is safe and effective. Again, use clean towels for each of these jobs. Don't mix your towels. Some people get different colored towels for different jobs to help them remember which is used for each application.

Time to clean the mirrors and any windscreen. Spray cleaning solution on towels, not the mirror or windshield, and that will give you more control here. It is best to avoid over-spraying.

Lastly, dress the wheels. I do NOT recommend that you dress your tires. Almost any substance on the market designed to make tires shiny will also cause them to have significantly reduced traction/grip. The LAST thing you want on a two-wheeled vehicle is loss of traction. So stick to the wheels. When cleaning the wheels use clean towels and if you have a bike jack, this is a great time to put the bike in the air so you can freely spin the wheels as you clean them.

CHAPTER SEVEN - FINISHING TOUCHES AND NEXT STEPS

"Catching a yellow jacket in your shirt at 70 mph can double your vocabulary."

After you've washed your bike and shined it up you're technically done. But the next step - if you want to take it - crosses over into what some people call detailing. These are the minute corrections to paint, polishes, sealants, and in some cases waxes that take your bike's finish to the next level.

I'm not going to get too deep into this subject, because frankly, that is an entire book all by itself. But I do want to touch on a few things that you can do to get your bike close to a professional detail without hiring the professional detailer.

It's called "detailing" because that is what you are looking for and working on - details. You might use a very small toothbrush for instance to clean between your engine fins. You will look for and remove minor scratches. This is where you get picky. Some people just don't see the value in cleaning their motorcycle this well. But I do.

The first step in the detailing process is taping off any decals or special areas where you've applied clear bra, etc. Polishes, sealants and waxes tend to build up on these edges so use low-tack race or detailing tape to tape these off. Overlap the just a little bit — maybe 1/8 of an inch. Next ,use a good quality-quick detail spray and clay bar to remove contaminants from the paint. Be

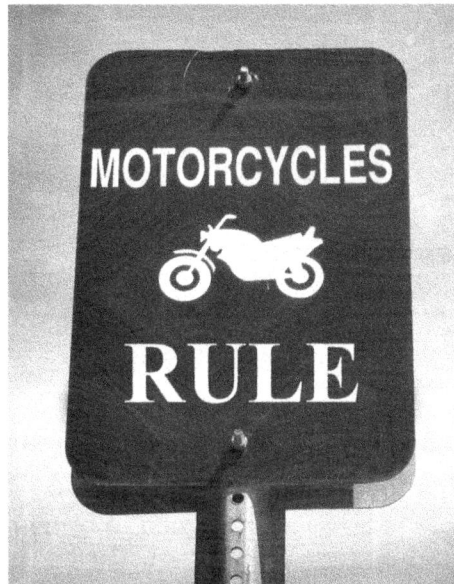

sure to flatten out your clay and use a quick-detail spray to provide lubrication. Work in a box - side-to-side and then top-to-bottom over a small section of the paint. Stretch, pull, and fold the clay bar over and over to bury the contaminants into the bar so you always have a fresh piece to work on your bike. If the clay bar starts to stick to your hand it's time to replace it. Likewise if you drop it on the ground, forget it. Throw it away and start over. Your paint is way more expensive than the clay bar. You can tell when you are done with the clay bar when the painted surfaces feel smooth to the touch. Always clay before you polish.

Next look for scratches. Deep scratches or serious paint flaws are beyond the scope of this book, but if you have small, minor scuffs or swirls you should be able to get them out with an inexpensive dual action buffer. While some people will advise you to try this with various chemicals and a towel or hand-held buffing pad, it's been my experience that the only way to really do this job well is with a buffer. Buffers generate heat and some of the better chemicals require this heat to activate.

Buffing out scratches is an art. But there's no need to be afraid of it. If you're using the tools I recommended above, and if you watch the short, free training videos I mentioned, then you should be able to tackle this fairly easily. If you've NEVER touched a buffer in your life, I suggest that you practice on an old hood, or fender from a vehicle you no longer use. This will build confidence and get you ready for the real job at hand. Note that if you decide to use a buffer other than a dual-action buffer, you do run a serious risk of permanently damaging your paint. Leave that work to full-time pros. When using a buffer make sure your polish and waxes are compatible. Chemical bases differ, and some chemicals react adversely when mixed.

After you have the scratches and swirls gone, try polishing your bike before or even instead of waxing it. Polish, followed by the right sealant, can provide as deep a shine and luster as most waxes. You should also know that polishes are designed to bring out your paint's best shine and waxes merely protect.

When you're polishing your bike, you can do this with a buffer, but unless you have experience using a buffer, I suggest adding the polish by hand.

Start with a high-quality polish. Check my recommendations in the tools chapter of the book. Apply the polish to your micro fiber cloth NOT the paint. In fact this is a good rule for most of the chemicals you use on your bike. Apply to a cloth first not the paint. Some polishes and other chemicals can leave stains if applied directly to the bike, especially if you haven't followed my advice to clean your bike in a cool, dry area.

Apply the polish according to the manufacturer's instructions, and then use a CLEAN micro fiber towel to remove it. Make sure you get ALL the polish buffed off the bike.

Nest step is sealant. Check my list above. Be careful not to use a sealant that seals the paint permanently. Paint needs to expand and contract with the temperature. Don't overdo the sealant. Sealers provide the ultimate in durability and protection. Sealers last the longest, are usually easier to use, and add a slippery and slick feel to your paint that is unlike that of natural carnauba car waxes.

Back to waxing: I am not against waxing a bike, but most of the time, people overpay for expensive waxes that don't last. Here's why — If you live in someplace where it gets very hot, the wax can literally melt off your bike. There are indeed waxes formulated with sophisticated polymers that resist heat. The really good ones can cost a fortune.

If you read the tools section you see that I will recommend one wax that is very affordable, and easy to apply. It even stands up to high heat most of the time. The Meguiar's wax protects your paint but for it to work properly, you must apply it properly. Use it very sparingly. Apply too much product and you get streaks. Better to have too little than too much.

It's particularly important to apply this product to a cool, dry surface. Seriously. This is a big deal. If it's hot or the surface isn't completely dry, you will not get good results with this or any other wax. Be sure to buff off the wax with a new, clean, micro fiber towel and be thorough. Another nice feature of the Meguiar's product is that you can apply it on top of old coats of wax without penalty. The fancy, expensive, Carnauba waxes need to be removed before you can apply a new coat.

There's one other product that I want to mention here because it came to my attention just as I was putting the finishing touches on this book. Stoner Speed Bead may be all the "detailing" your motorcycle ever needs. It's more effective than the Meguiar's product but it requires just a touch more work. You spray it on, let it set for a minute, and then buff it off. What the Stoner's product does is nothing short of magic. It actually does everything from clean the bike, to remove water spots, and even fill in micro abrasions (if used properly.) It is in almost every way as good as a hand wax and it's less than $10. In case you don't believe me, try it. You'll change your mind just as I did. I was very skeptical but just "detailed" my bike, my truck and my trailer in under three hours using Speed Bead. The only thing that you need to be careful with when using Speed Bead is that you need to be very thorough when removing it, otherwise it will leave a little dust residue. It won't go quite as deep as a hand wax, but unless you're entering your bike in a concours event who cares?

http://amzn.to/1aSWjy3

The money you paid for this book will be well spent if you just take this one piece of advice. Don't go crazy spending a fortune on wax. I just don't see the difference most of the time and the cost (both in time and money) is, in my opinion, never worth the result. Avoid the boutique waxes. Stick with the products I suggest and you can call it a day.

Chapter 8 - MAINTAINING YOUR BIKE'S SEAT

"You might be a biker if: Your bike is in the living room and your couch is on the patio."

We can't forget the seat. After all, it's where you literally park yourself every time you ride. Most of you will have leather seats. Some seats are made of synthetic leather or even vinyl. The same sorts of products and techniques will work on any of the above.

Even if the seat doesn't look like it's dirty, you should clean it. Most seats are black and black hides dirt well. Instead of an oily compound designed for shine, try a vinyl or leather cleaner. You might be surprised by how much grime comes off, and the seat won't be slippery.

As you prepare to clean seats, start by ensuring you have the proper product for the job. You'll want to have a high-quality leather cleaner with a neutral ph to avoid damaging leather seats' dyes and oils. If you have a seat that is stained, you may have re-dye it to cover the stain or fix minor wear.

For upholstered seats, vacuuming may be sufficient on a regular basis but at some point you'll want to clean carpets and seats with stain remover and cleaning solution. Periodically, it's a good idea to apply protectants to leather and vinyl surfaces.

Use a soft sponge or towel to clean, taking care to get into all the crevices and raise the headrest to access the top of the seat. Follow up with a clean, dry towel to remove excess liquid.

Depending on the condition of the seats, apply leather cleaner or stain remover for upholstered seats first and then use a cleaning solution. Extract the chemicals with a wet-dry vac or extractor and then follow up by spraying a very small amount of clean water over the area to rinse. Extract the rinse water using the wet-dry vac or an extractor. It's important to avoid over soaking the seats and remove as much of the cleaning chemicals as possible because cleaning residue will attract dirt. Work from the top down so that drips will be removed as you proceed down.

CHAPTER 9 - KEEPING YOUR BIKE CLEAN AFTER THE WASH

"I'd rather be riding my motorcycle thinking about God than sitting in church thinking about my motorcycle"

Old sayings are old sayings because they are generally true. An ounce of prevention is indeed worth a pound of cure. If you want the job of maintaining your motorcycle's appearance to be easier next time, you can take steps now to make sure next time's wash goes more smoothly.

Sunlight is the enemy of paint, leather, and vinyl. If possible keep your bike in a garage, under a carport or otherwise indoors. If you aren't married you can possibly get away with pulling it into the living room! Not only does this protect the bike's finish, but it reduces chances of theft.

If you can't keep your bike indoors, you can use a bike cover but in my experience, they all most always cause fine scratches on the motorcycle sooner or later. If you do invest in a bike cover get the best one you can afford. That will reduce scratches in the paint when you pull it on or off.

Avoid riding through sprinklers (hard water) or in the center of your lane where all the oil and debris from the car in front of you is being dropped.

Make sure that YOU don't cause damage to your bike by wearing clothing or accessories that are likely to scratch the bike or damage the leather. Belt buckles do more damage to motorcycles than accidents. Even plastic rain suits can scuff your paint. The most likely place you'll cause damage is on the gas tank, where the seat and the tank meet. Be extra careful in this area.

Consider using clear bra to protect the most exposed surfaces of your bike. There is a down side to this decision. Clear bra (when done right) is very expensive and has its own problems. It attracts dust and the edges can get gummed up with dirt. But in some cases, I have seen bikes benefit from the proper application of a high-quality clear bra.

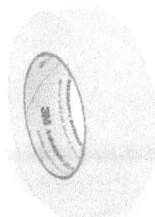

Use racing tape if you take your bike off road or onto the track. This is a low-tack tape that is designed for use in auto body shops but works great for taping off fairings, headlights, etc that might be exposed to rock chips in an off-road or racing situation. I use 3M 06654 36 mm x 55 m Automotive Refinish Masking Tape. It comes in different widths. Be sure to take it off as soon as you can. Leaving it on over night isn't the worst thing in the world, but it will leave more residue. The good news is that you can easily remove tape residue by using an instant detailer and micro-fiber towel.

Wash your bike every one to two weeks to keep it looking its best. If you go too long between washes, you can actually make it harder to bring the bike back to its best shine.

You can also do some spot cleaning in between washes. Once you've created a fresh, pristine shine, you can keep it up with a detailing spray. These sprays are a great way to stay on top of any fingerprint smudges around the door handles or random bug splats or dust. Be sure to spray the liquid cleaners on a clean towel before wiping on the bike. You'll find some of these products even come in travel sizes and wet wipes that are handy for when you're out and about town or on a long road trip. (See above.)

BONUS CHAPTER 10 - *Sage Advice*

Never ride behind a garbage truck. I'm just saying.

Thanks for buying the book. I hope it helps and if you have questions, comments, or concerns please feel free to contact me at scotty@bigscotty.com. Keep the shiny side up!

Published by BigScotty.com

Copyright 2014, All Rights Reserved - For permissions contact scotty@bigscotty.com

ISBN-13:

978-0615960777 (BigScotty.com)

ISBN-10:

0615960774

For More Information Contact:

BigScotty.com

8100 Wyoming Blvd. Ste M4#349

Albuquerque, NM 87113

info@bigscotty.com